Editor
Charlene Stout

Editorial Project Manager
Ina Massler Levin, M.A.

Editor-in-Chief
Sharon Coan, M.S. Ed.

Illustrator
Barb Lorseydi

Cover Artists
Sue Fullam
Jose L. Tapia

Art Coordination Assistant
Cheri Macoubrie Wilson

Art Director
Elayne Roberts

Imaging
Alfred Lau
Ralph Olmedo, Jr.

Production Manager
Phil Garcia

Publisher
Mary D. Smith, M.S. Ed.

How to Write a Research Report

Grades 3-6

Author

Kathleen Christopher Null

Teacher Created Resources, Inc.
6421 Industry Way
Westminster, CA 92683
www.teachercreated.com
©*1998 Teacher Created Resources, Inc.*
Reprinted, 2007
Made in U.S.A.
ISBN 13: 978-1-57690-332-2

Table of Contents

Introduction

When a teacher posts "How to Write a Research Report" under assignments, the most universal reaction is an audible groan. Only recently have we evolved from years of English books, actually grammar books, devoted to correct expression and format, reserving the last chapter for writing a paragraph or essay. *How to Write a Research Report* takes students through all the basic steps necessary to bring a topic through all the "work in progress" stages from researching through "souping up" the presentation. A note to parents suggests appropriate support and sets important step-by-step due dates for each phase in the "construction project." In the end, don't be surprised if your students conclude, "Research reports are rad!"

This book is divided into the following sections:

Getting Started

Students will learn what a research report is and receive writing prompts to warm up their writing muscles. They will investigate reference books and other resources that are available and then choose a workable topic and ask the important questions, Who? What? When? Where? Why? and How?

Using the Library

Students will explore the library, learning to use the Dewey Decimal System, periodicals, encyclopedias, almanacs, atlases, dictionaries, vertical files, multimedia collections, bibliographies, and computer resources.

Taking Notes

Students will narrow the focus of a report by writing a main idea card before beginning their search for information. They will discover the note-taking process and the ease of using index cards to organize and track information.

Saving Data

Students will practice how to write an outline and keep their notes, charts, lists, diagrams, and pictures close at hand as a blueprint for quickly getting their ideas on paper.

Getting It in Shape

Students will learn the steps of the writing process, the importance of editing and documenting, and the use of guidelines to format (plan and organize) their report.

At Last—Writing the Report!

Students will study examples and complete exercises for the various parts of the report.

Souping Up the Report

Students will learn to creatively enhance a report with auditory, visual, and tactile products that will clarify and add sparkle to their presentations.

What Is a Research Report?

A research report presents information that the writer has learned through a detective-like search for the facts. Facts are found in books, magazines, newspapers, encyclopedias, atlases, computer programs, even in personal interviews. As you collect the best facts to write your report, you become an expert on your topic.

How do you choose a subject? Your teacher may have you choose from a list of subjects related to something you have been studying. Or, your teacher may ask you to choose a topic of particular interest to you and have it approved. To be sure you have plenty of information available, you might want to choose three topics. Then check in the library to see how much information you can find on each before you decide on the one topic for your report. If your topic has so much information that it is overwhelming, you may need to narrow it down.

In the box of possible topics below, circle all those that interest you.

bears	rivers
spiders	deserts
horses	mountains
reptiles	caves
giraffes	track
whales	basketball
jets	swimming
missiles	soccer
boats	tennis
trains	hiking
cars	camping
motorcycles	fishing
lakes	rafting
oceans	canoeing

Choose three favorite topics from above and write them on the lines below. After each, write a more specific topic that might make your report more manageable.

Favorite Topic	**More Specific Topic**
Example: Planets	Mars
1. _____	_____
2. _____	_____
3. _____	_____

Choosing a Subject

Pretend your teacher has given you a list of subject ideas. You have chosen the subject "Mammals" as the one that interests you most. Now what? You'd better get busy right away!

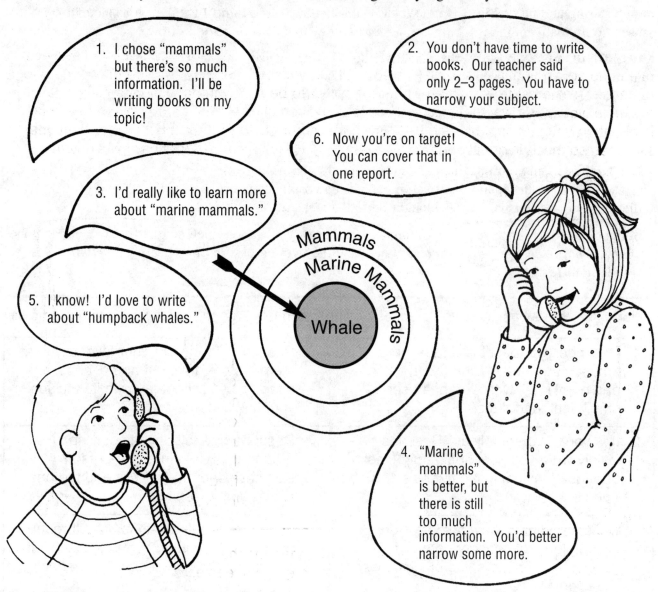

1. I chose "mammals" but there's so much information. I'll be writing books on my topic!

2. You don't have time to write books. Our teacher said only 2–3 pages. You have to narrow your subject.

6. Now you're on target! You can cover that in one report.

3. I'd really like to learn more about "marine mammals."

5. I know! I'd love to write about "humpback whales."

Mammals
Marine Mammals
Whale

4. "Marine mammals" is better, but there is still too much information. You'd better narrow some more.

Now it's your turn to narrow down these subjects.

Chosen Topic	Narrowed Down	Narrowed Down More
Transportation	_____	_____
Insects	_____	_____
Holidays	_____	_____
Plants	_____	_____
National Parks	_____	_____

Writing Prompts

Have you ever stared at a blank piece of paper with no clue about where to start and what to write? Well, you are not alone. Even if you are writing a research paper with a stack of notes, you can still end up staring at a blank page. Don't worry. This can be a good thing. Think of it as a creativity pause. Your creative mind is taking a time-out to allow the ideas to begin to flow.

A research report deserves your best creative ideas. For instance, your report on African elephants will be very dull if you merely organize your facts and begin writing. If you pause, you might visualize the powerful animals moving across a dusty plain, trumpeting loudly, kicking up a dust cloud that dries your nose and throat, causing the ground to vibrate. When you pause, your researched facts and your imagination can combine to produce sensory images. Your report on African Elephants can captivate your audience with clear, visual images in addition to the facts.

Before you begin to write your report, think of the basics you want to include: the five W's and the one H: *Who, What, Where, When, Why, and How?* and the five senses: *Hearing, Seeing, Smelling, Touching, and Tasting.*

Include the above basics as you practice writing warm-ups with the following writing prompts:

1. Describe your best trip to a favorite amusement park. Using the five W's and one H, tell what you hear, see, smell, feel, and taste.	6. Describe picking out your favorite pet at the pet store, taking it home, and spending your first day with it. Include your five senses.
2. It is your favorite holiday. Describe vividly what you see, hear, smell, feel, and taste, including the five W's and one H.	7. Describe one full day of your trip around the world in a one-person sailboat. Use the five W's and the one H and all the senses.
3. Describe your all-time favorite story. Using plenty of sensory details, tell about the characters, the places, and the events.	8. Take a new friend who is blind through your day, describing everything so well that he or she can sense it all perfectly.
4. Recall a special time at a favorite place to visit. Include the five W's and one H, telling what you see, hear, smell, touch, and taste there.	9. Describe a hike through a canyon full of wild animals, using the W's and one H and your senses as you encounter four of the animals.
5. Describe a funny thing that happened to you or someone you know. Use your senses as you tell the five W's and one H.	10. You have invented a futuristic vehicle. Describe your "craft" and your trip out into the great unknown.

A Note for Parents

Dear Parent: Date _____

I am writing a research report on _____.

The final report is due on _____. However, before the final report is

turned in, I need to have my teacher check off that the following requirements are each

completed on the following dates:

    The outline is due in class on _____.

    The note cards are due in class on _____.

    The table of contents is due in class on _____.

    The bibliography is due in class on _____.

Please help me complete this project by taking me to the library, by encouraging

and supervising my research, and by assisting me with pictures, graphs, maps, etc.

Thank you for your interest and encouragement on this project. Please sign the tear-off below
so that I can return it to my teacher tomorrow.

_____

(signature of student)

_____ I have read the research report notice and discussed it with my son or daughter.

_____ I will encourage and supervise him or her in the timely completion of each part of this
assignment.

_____ I wish to have a conference regarding this assignment.

_____   _____

(parent's signature)   (date)

Exploring the Library

Since ancient times libraries have been storage places for the collected knowledge and wisdom of the world. There are public libraries, school libraries, college and university libraries, state libraries, technical libraries (such as medical, law, science, and engineering libraries), and reference libraries for rare, old, fragile, valuable books.

Most of your research will be done in libraries, so it is important to learn your way around them. Once you understand how the Dewey Decimal System works, you will have no problem finding any subject you want. You'll also find magazines, newspapers, audio and video tapes, pamphlets, and computer software. In the reference section of each library are several books titled *The Reader's Guide to Periodical Literature* which list magazine articles written about your subject.

The librarians at each library have studied library science. They are experts in finding information on any subject. Their purpose is to assist library visitors. Do not hesitate to ask them for help.

Follow the three pathways on the Library map (page 9) for practice in finding your way around a library while searching for information on each of these three topics:

Hunting Dogs

- Ask the librarian for help finding books about hunting dogs.
- On the shelves find four books with information on hunting dogs.
- Ask the librarian where you can find more information on hunting dogs.
- Look in the *Reader's Guide* for magazines that contain information.
- Go to the magazine section and find three magazines with articles on hunting dogs.
- Take the four books and three magazines to a quiet study area and take notes.

Native American Foods

- Use the card catalog to find the Dewey Decimal numbers on this subject.
- Find two cookbooks with authentic Native American recipes.
- From the computer catalog get the numbers for three books on Native Americans.
- Find the books on the shelves. Check indexes and tables of contents.
- Look in the *Reader's Guide* and find hundreds of magazine articles.
- Call Mom to bring your pillow, blanket, and toothbrush!

Snowboarding

- Use the computer catalog. Write down the numbers for books on the subject.
- Look in the *Reader's Guide* for magazine articles on snowboarding.
- Go to the shelves and find the four best books on snowboarding
- Search the magazine section for the best magazine articles on snowboarding.
- Choose the best three magazines and two books that you found on the subject.
- Take them to a desk where you can work quietly taking notes.

Library Pathways

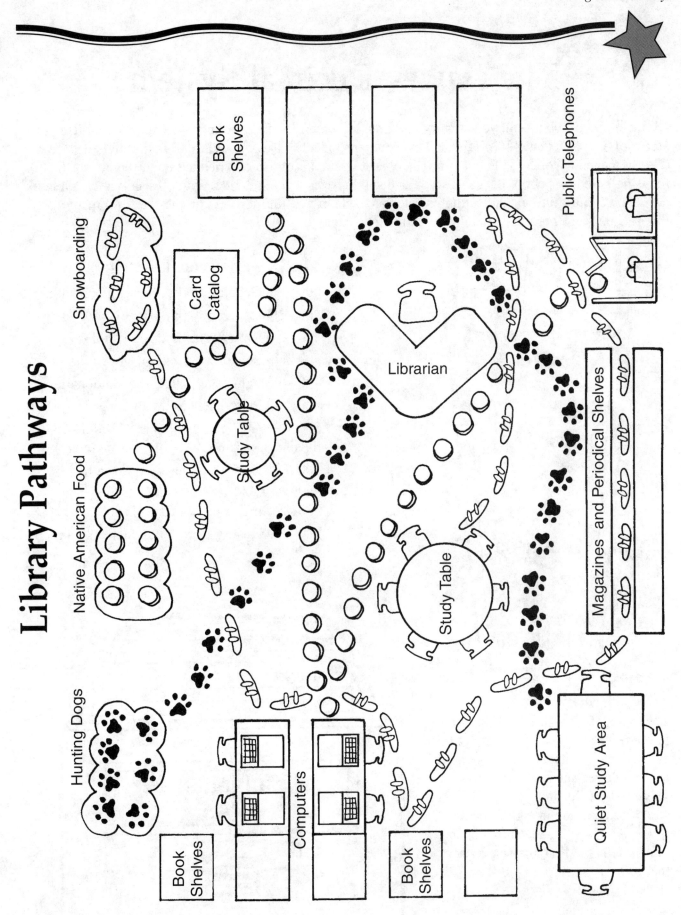

The Dewey Decimal System

All the nonfiction books in your library are arranged according to a number system called the **Dewey Decimal System** created by a famous librarian named Melvil Dewey. It has 10 major divisions from 000 for General Works to the 900s for History. Each major division is divided into 10 parts, each focusing on one aspect of the category. Each subdivision is again divided into 10 sections. Each book has its own **call number**, indicating its category, to help you find it easily on the shelf. In many libraries this information is found on a computer system.

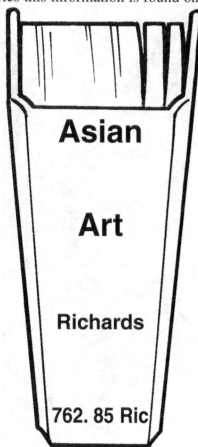

Asian

Art

Richards

762. 85 Ric

The Dewey Decimal System

000–099 General Works (encyclopedia, atlas)

100–199 Philosophy (philosophy, psychology)

200–299 Religion (religions, mythology)

300–399 Social Science (law, government)

400–499 Language (languages, dictionaries)

500–599 Pure Sciences (math, biology, space)

600–699 Applied Sciences and Useful Arts (business, farming, cooking, cosmetology)

700–799 Fine Arts (music, sports, art, photography)

800–899 Literature (poetry, plays)

900–999 History (travel, biography, geography,)

The Card Catalog

The index of all of the books in the library is kept on cards in drawers that can be easily updated. Each book is listed on three separate cards, by **subject**, by **title**, and by **author**. The cards are arranged in alphabetical order. The label on the front of each drawer tells the first and last cards in that drawer.

Subjects
A–Ac

The Dewey Decimal System *(cont.)*

When you know a book's **call number**, it is easy to locate it quickly. To find the call number, look in the library **card catalog** for the author's name, the book's title, or the book's subject. (The numbers are the category group and the letters Dor are the beginning letters of the author's name. J or X means the book is found in the children's section. YA means young adult section.)

Read and discuss the similarities and differences among the three cards below:

Subject Card
Subject
J 629.132 Dor
Aeronautics—Accident Investigation
Dorman, Michael F.
Detectives of the Sky; Investigating Aviation Accidents. Watts. c 1976. Index. Biblio.

Title Card
Title
J 629.132 Dor
Detectives of the Sky
Dorman, Michael F.
Detectives of the Sky; Investigating Aviation Accidents. Watts. c 1976.

Author Card
Author
Dorman, Michael F.
J 629.132 Dor
Includes index. Describes the work of government investigators of airplane crashes, citing types of accidents and specific crashes.
Bibliography: p. 97
Subject Heading
1. Aeronautics—Accident investigation.

Finding Books on Library Shelves

Public Library

000-099 General Works (magazines, newspaper, enclyopedia, atlas, multimedia	6th
100-199 Philosophy (psychology) 200-299 Religion (mythology)	5th
300-399 Social Science (law, government) 400-499 Language (dictionaries)	4th
500-599 Pure Sciences (space, mathematics) 600-699 Applied Sciences (cooking, media)	3rd
700-799 Fine Arts (architecture, sculpting, music, photography, recreation, sports)	2nd
800-899 Literature (novels, poetry, plays) 900-999 History and Geography (travel)	1st

Using the information above, chart the following ten topics. Are any found in more than one place? _____

Topic	Category	Subdivision	Shelf Number	Floor
1. baseball	Fine Arts	sports	700–799	2nd
2. poems				
3. maps				
4. rock bands				
5. fractions				
6. Abe Lincoln				
7. thesaurus				
8. voting				
9. barbeque				
10. Hercules				

On another paper, chart five subjects of interest to you. In the library card catalog, find one book about each subject on your list. Write the title, call number, and shelf number for each of the five books. Then try to find all five books on the shelves.

	Subject	Title	Call Number	Shelf Number
1.				
2.				
3.				
4.				
5.				

Finding Books on Library Shelves (cont.)

All nonfiction books are arranged on the library shelves in number order from left to right.

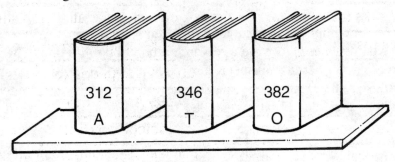

If any books have exactly the same Dewey Decimal number, they are arranged alphabetically by the initials of the authors' last names.

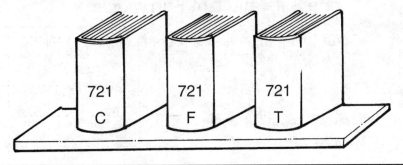

It is your turn to write the call numbers in the correct order on these library books. Remember to go from left to right in number order. Also, use alphabetical order if the numbers are the same.

592	530	581	546	501	579	530
N	B	C	I	K	P	T

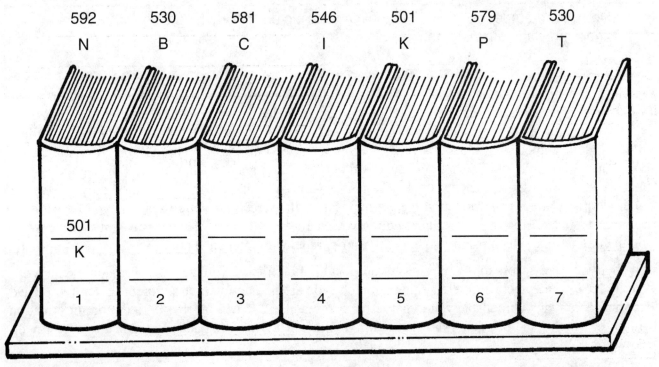

Researching on the Internet

As Robert Louis Stevenson says, "The world is full of a number of things . . . " and they can all be found on the Internet!

The Internet is a network of computers that are all connected so they can "talk" to each other. For example, ten-year-old Matthew needs to write a research report about life on the Mississippi River during the times of Tom Sawyer because his class just read the book *The Adventures of Tom Sawyer*. Since Matt is at school using the computer lab, he decides to look up his topic on the Internet. He manages to connect with a university library in another state and finds more information than he can use.

Sounds great! However, before you go "online," keep in mind some important safety rules.

Be Safe and Not Sorry Online

1. Never give any personal information about yourself or your family, such as your full name, where you live, or your telephone number.

2. You will meet many friendly people online, but remember—they are strangers.

3. If you find yourself having an online conversation that makes you uncomfortable report that person to your online service.

4. Don't give away your password.

5. Don't agree to meet anyone you've chatted with online unless your parents agree to the meeting and go with you to a public place.

6. Don't send someone you've met online your picture or anything else without first checking with your parents.

Online, at the click of a mouse, you can find dictionaries, encyclopedias, newsstands (current news from many newspapers), magazine data bases, homework helpers, and a variety of other references. To find the answer to a question such as, "What's the longest river in the world?" you could use an online program like "Homework Helper" by Prodigy. Simply type your question and tell the program where to search: "Look in books." Click on **Search** and the program goes to work looking through its database for anything that matches the key words *longest, river,* and *world*. It will probably offer a hundred or so sources of information that will appear on the screen for you to scan. If you find a long article that is useful for you, you can save it on your hard drive to read later. That way it won't cost you the online time which can be expensive. Your parents will appreciate that.

Whether you have access to the Internet at your local public library, your school, or at home, you will want to have some practice in researching a topic if you are new to Internet research. Even if you have experience, practice will enable you to get faster at research. You will be able to find more information within the time limitations necessary when going online. The following activity (page 15) will provide you with practice.

Surfing for Information

To help you learn to surf the Internet for information, your teacher will assign you a topic to research and show you how to use a "search engine."

What You Need:

Hardware:

IBM, Macintosh, or compatible computer with a connection to the Internet

Software:

either a Web browsing program such as Netscape or Mosaic or a commercial online account that supports the World Wide Web

Surf Research Form (below)

What You Do:

1. Brainstorm your assigned topic.

2. Make a list of subtopics.
   Topic: *Bears;* Subtopics: *environment, feeding habits, behavior*

3. Use a search engine to research your topic and subtopics to find information.

4. With your teacher's permission, choose which documents to print and which to save, and create a file of information to use later.

Surf Research Form

Directions: Use an Internet search engine to find information about your topic. Make sure that you focus on the subtopics. Print the information that covers the topic. List your sources.

Name _____ Date _____

Topic: _____

Subtopics: A. _____

B. _____

C. _____

D. _____

I will use _____ as my search engine(s) to find sites about my topic.

Internet Sites Used: _____

Name of the Site _____Type of Site:_____

URL of the Site (site address): _____

Researching Periodicals

Periodicals are simply magazines and newspapers which are published periodically—monthly, weekly, and daily. When you can't find enough books on your subject, such as "Snowboarding," turn to the periodicals section of the library. Because they are published so frequently, they often have the most current information on a subject. Here's what you do:

1. In the library's reference section, find *The Reader's Guide to Periodical Literature* which lists the latest magazine articles.

2. Look up your subject. Select the most informative articles. Jot down the titles, dates, and volume numbers of the magazines you want, or print out a copy.

3. Give that information to the librarians in the periodicals section. They will help you find those periodicals.

Most public libraries have this same information on their computers for library cardholders. It is called the **Public Access Catalog,** and it lists both books and periodicals. In some libraries, your own personal computer can have access to this catalog, giving you information about adult books, children's fiction and nonfiction books, periodicals, videos, and CDs, all available in many languages. Ask your librarian for an informational brochure about their online Public Access Catalog.

Read and discuss these entries about "Dogs" from the computer's online public catalog:

Database: General Reference Center

Subject: Dogs

Subdivision: Care and Treatment

Library: Orange County Public Library

"Making the Dog Days Longer." (Preventive health care for pets) (T&C's Guide to Veterinary Medicine) Kate Johanna Weiner. *Town & Country Monthly*, July 1997 v151 n5206 p 114 (1). Mag. Coll.: 8965477. Elec. Coll.: A19550558.

—Abstract and Text Available—

"Tails of Woe: the Shocking Truth About Puppy Mills." Alison Bell. *Teen Magazine*. June 1997 v41 n6 p71(3). Elec. Coll.: A19661336.

—Abstract and Text Available—

"Out of Harm's Way: Knowing Simple First-aid Tips Could Save Your Pet's Life." Elizabeth Leaff. *Saturday Evening Post*, March–April 1996 v268 n2 p26(3). Mag. Call.: 82L155. Elec. Coll A18049424.

—Abstract and Text Available—

Using Encyclopedia Volumes

An encyclopedia is a set of books which contains information on just about everything in the world. The information is arranged in alphabetical order, beginning with the A's in the first volume and ending with the Z's in the last volume. Your library will have an encyclopedia; it may have several. Your school library will probably have one, too. An encyclopedia is a good place to find information for your research paper.

Write each of the subjects below on the spine of the encyclopedia volume in which they would be found.

photography	rattlesnakes	The Beatles
dinosaurs	lightning	volcanoes
Hawaii	wildflowers	space shuttle
chocolate	computers	gorillas

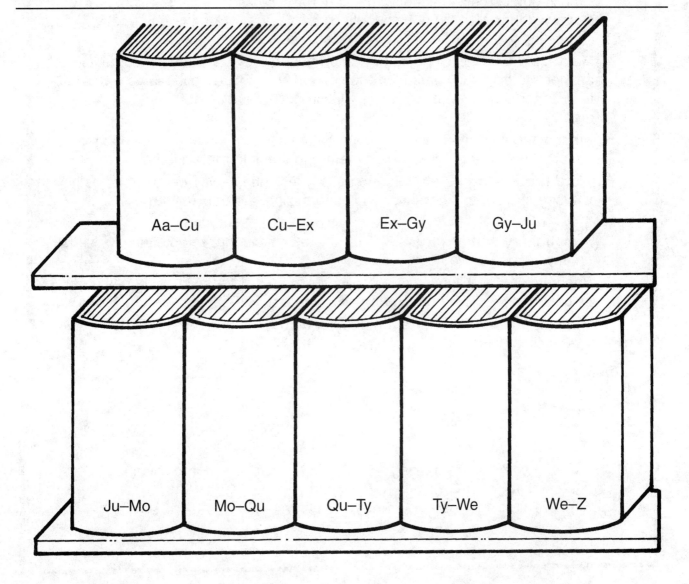

Using Computer Encyclopedias

If your school or library has a computer with a CD-ROM (compact disk-read only memory) drive, you will have access to an amazing amount of information that is only a mouse click away. Here's what you do, one step at a time:

1. Place the encyclopedia **disk** in the **drive**, close the drawer, and follow the instructions on the screen to open the program.

2. When you get to the **main menu**, you can click on a guided **tour** or **tutorial** (or both) to find introductory demonstrations that will give you helpful information in your explorations.

3. The main menu will also offer you at least two ways to start your **search**. (1) You can type your subject into a box and then click "get item," "article," or simply "get" or "find." Instantly, the screen will fill with the information. (2) You can scroll through a list of alphabetized topics and click on one that is interesting to you. When it is highlighted, you can click "get" or "find."

4. Many CD-ROM encyclopedias will allow you to click on a table of contents or an index to help you search for a topic, or you can type an idea into a box to find related topics. Most will have a list of books to read at the end of the article.

5. When your topic information appears on the screen, you can scroll and read the articles or insert bookmarks to return to that information later.

6. **Word processing notebooks** are usually included so you can take notes as you search. You can **copy** your notes to a clipboard to **print out** or use in another program.

7. A **dictionary** or **thesaurus** is also likely to be included, so you can easily look up any words that you don't know.

8. Bright-colored highlighting of some words in an article (such as names and places) can be clicked on to bring up another article about the same topic.

9. You may find **tables, charts, time lines, maps, sound,** and **animation** for use in a multimedia report.

Spend some time exploring a CD-ROM encyclopedia for topics that interest you. Jot down where they lead you—tables? charts? maps? time lines? sound? other topics?

Card and Computer Catalogs

Each library has catalogs to help you find the books you want. One is called the "card catalog." It is a cabinet of small file drawers which contains cards for each book in the library. Each card has a "call number" that helps you find the book on the shelf. The "computer catalog" contains the same information and much more. The librarians are happy to teach you to use these catalogs.

In the card catalog you will find that each book has three cards which are filed alphabetically. The **title cards** are filed by the titles of the books. A card for *Green Eggs and Ham* can be found in the "G" drawer. The **author cards** list the books by the authors' last names. If your author is Scott O'Dell, you will find his card filed in the "O" drawer. If you don't know the author's name or the book title but know that you want to find books on "whales," you can find the **subject cards** for whales in the "W" drawer. Be sure you write down all of the books' call numbers.

The computer catalog works like a card catalog. You can type what you know—author, subject, or title—and wait while the computer does the searching for you. Soon you will see your author's name, the book's title, the subject, and a list of other books by the same author. If you type in the subject, you will find a list of other books on the same or similar subjects. The computer will also list the book's call number, state how many copies are available in the library, and tell if the book you want is still on the shelf.

Here is a list of titles, authors, and subjects. You need more information. After each item on the list, write whether you need to look up the book on a **title card**, an **author card**, or a **subject card**.

The Napping House _____

oceans _____

skiing _____

Mark Twain _____

The Black Stallion _____

India _____

The Bridge to Terabithia _____

computers _____

Theodore Taylor _____

Island of the Blue Dolphins _____

Information Sources

Use this form to record sources of information for your topic, such as encyclopedia articles, books, magazines, newspapers, computer encyclopedias, Internet, etc. If you are unable to find very many sources, see your teacher right away. You may need to choose another topic. Take this form with you when you look up your topic. Be sure to have your teacher check it before you begin your research.

Name _____ Topic_____

Write the names and volumes of encyclopedias you find useful.

Encyclopedia

_____

Volume/Page

_____

Write the titles, authors, and call numbers of books you find useful.

Title

_____

Author_____ Call number _____

Use *The Reader's Guide to Periodical Literature* for magazine information.

Article Title _____

Publication _____ Date _____

Write the names of computer encyclopedias containing helpful information and the article titles that you found.

Encyclopedia Name

_____

Title of Article

_____

List Web sites found that contain helpful information on your topic.

Name of site_____

URL (WWW Address) _____

Clustering Ideas

Clustering is a creative prewriting exercise to help you organize your information so you can see how the parts fit together. Clustering is sometimes called *webbing* or *mapping*. As you search and research your topic, jot down the subtopics you want to include in the form shown below. Start with the large center circle for the main topic. All around it, attach subtopic circles. Around them, cluster the pieces of information in the correct subtopic.

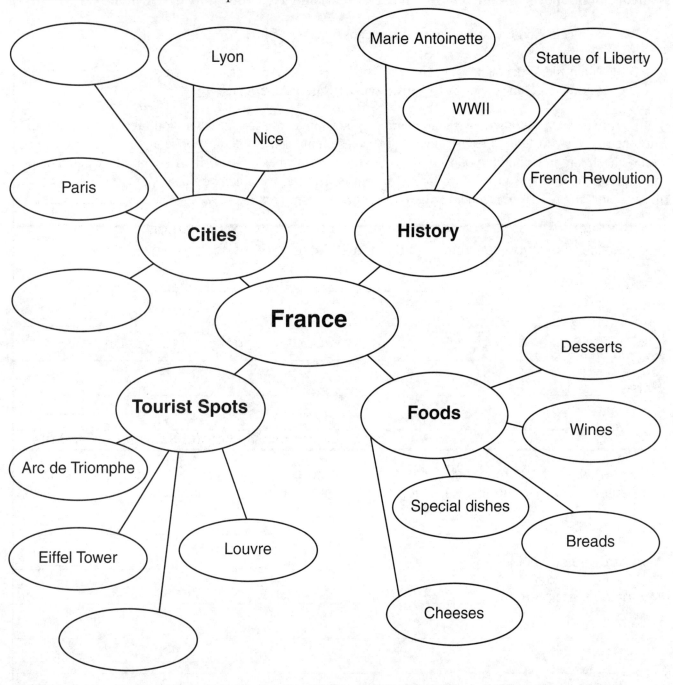

On the back of this page, cluster your note card topics to help you organize your report.

The Main Idea Statement

After you have chosen a topic and done a little research, you will probably have a good idea what your report will be about. This is a good time to create a main idea statement. It will save you time because you will be able to focus on your topic and avoid taking unnecessary notes.

Your main idea statement will be the first sentence of your report. All your notes and every sentence that follows in your report will need to be connected with your first sentence.

> Subject: Southwestern Native Americans
> Narrowed Subject: The Anasazi
> Main Idea Statement: The Anasazi, known as "The Ancient Ones," were a highly developed and prosperous group of Native Americans.

Put your main idea statement on the top card of your note cards so that when you take notes, you will stay focused on your main idea. If your main idea statement was the one above about the Anasazi, you could check any information you find about Southwestern tribes to see if it will support that statement. Information about the Anasazi's well-constructed homes, for example, would support it while information about a Hopi legend would not support it.

For practice, see if you can write a main idea statement for the topics below.

Basketball _____

Space _____

Computers _____

Horses _____

Ice Cream _____

Now narrow down your subject. Think carefully before you write your main idea statement. Remember, it will be the first sentence of your report and all sentences support it.

My subject is _____

My narrowed subject is _____

My main idea statement _____

_____

_____

_____

Have your teacher check your main idea statement before you go any further.

Writing Note Cards

A packet of index cards can be your best friend when you begin to write your research paper. If you do a good job of writing the note cards, you will be able to sort and rearrange your notes without needing to go back to look up information.

Materials

- a set of index cards (any size)
- a pen or pencil
- thick rubber band or envelope
- page 24 for sample note cards

Directions

1. Keep your stack of cards handy so you can add to your notes easily.

2. On the top card write **your name**, **the topic,** and **the date**.

3. On the next card, (the source card) write **source # "1" in the top, right-hand corner**. The source is where the information came from. The number will change as the source changes.

4. Write the **key word in the upper left-hand corner** of your card. This key word will be a subtopic for your report. If you are writing a report on baseball, whenever you find information on the history of baseball, you would write the key word *History* in the left corner of that card before you write the information. To organize your notes, you will be able to make a stack of all the cards about baseball history.

5. Next on this card you will write the **name of the source** (usually the author's full name), the **title** of the book or article, the **date and place of publication**, and the **page numbers**. You have to write the information about the publication only one time. After that just write the same source number on a card to know which book the information came from.

6. The rest of your card should be used to record the information you need for your report. Be sure to use quotation marks for quotations and use your own words for the rest. If you have more notes from the same book, use another card and write the same source number, the pages, and the information.

7. When you take notes from another book, give it the next source number and record the author's name, the book title and the publishing information on the first card from that source, as you did with the first one.

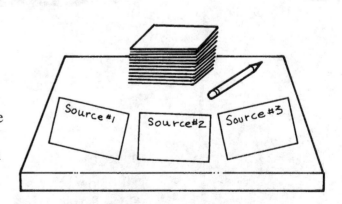

8. Be sure to keep all your note cards because you will use them for writing every part of your report, even the bibliography at the end.

Writing Note Cards *(cont.)*

Sample Note Cards

(The Top Card)

Sean Peters

Football

September 29

(The First Card for the First Source)

History   1

    Conklin, Mike.

    Inside Football

    Contemporary, 1978

    pages 26–30

    In the 1820's rugby came from soccer in England.

    American football came from rugby.

(Second Card from the Same First Source)

History   1

    Footballs used to be made from an animal's bladder.

    page 31

(A Card from a New or Second Source)

Professional Football   2

    Hollander, Zander, *The Complete Handbook of Pro Football,* 14th ed.

    NAL, 1988

    page 16

    The oldest major bowl game is the Rose Bowl.

Organizing Notes

You've read endless books, magazine articles, and encyclopedias. You're suffering from "mouse finger" after hours of clicking at the computer. You've got piles of note cards and chronic writer's cramp. What's next? It's time to organize your notes and create a rough outline.

1. Check each note card and eliminate any that do not match up with your main idea statement.

2. Sort your note cards into piles of related information. For example, if your report is about **grizzly bears**, sort your note cards so that one pile is about the *origins* and *history* of grizzlies, one pile is information about the bear's *diet*, one pile is information about the bear's *behavior*, etc.

3. Once your cards are sorted, arrange the piles in order. You may want to begin with the *early history* of the bear, where and when it was first found, etc. Put that pile of cards aside to be first in your written report and look for the next logical subtopic.

4. If you come across a pile that has only a little bit of information, you have the following choices: include it in another pile, do more research, or toss it out if it wasn't important anyway.

5. When you have your cards in order, you can write a rough "outline." Give one heading for each pile of cards and briefly list the bits of information about each as subtopics.

Study this example of a rough outline before writing your own on page 26.

Subject: The grizzly bears of Wyoming

Part I. History and origins   (your first pile of cards)

   Subtopics: where the first grizzly was sighted–How the bear got its name–Where the bear came from–cousins and other animal relatives

Part II. Hunting the Grizzly (your second pile of cards)

   Subtopics: trappers and fur traders–grizzly products–human encounters–the endangerment of the grizzly bear.

Organizing Notes *(cont.)*

Now it's your turn. Arrange your note cards in order and sort them into piles of subtopics. Write a rough outline using the form below and continuing on the back of this page if needed. Once they are in outline order, number all your cards, so the information will be in the order you want to write your report.

Name _____

Subject of Report: _____

Part I: _____

    Subtopics:_____

Part II: _____

    Subtopics:_____

Part III: _____

    Subtopics:_____

Part IV: _____

    Subtopics:_____

Part V: _____

    Subtopics:_____

Part VI: _____

    Subtopics:_____

Part VII: _____

    Subtopics:_____

Outlining

An outline is like a blueprint or a recipe. Once you have written your outline, writing your report will be a piece of cake! You can use your note cards to help you decide how to arrange your outline. Go through your note cards and sort them according to their subtopics—your key word in the upper left-hand corner of the card. (Pages 25 and 26 provided good practice in organizing notes.)

Below is a sample of the final outline for a research report on dogs. Notice that all the main topics are to the left and have the Roman numerals of I., II., etc. The subtopics are indented and have the capital letters of A., B., C., etc. The details under each subtopic are also indented and have Arabic numerals and finally, the lowercase letters of a., b., c., etc. give details about the Arabic numerals items.

Dogs

Dogs in today's society have two roles: working dogs and house pets.

I. Working Dogs

  A. Hunting

    1. Retrievers

      a. Golden

      b. Labrador

    2. Terriers

      a. Jack Russell

      b. Wirehaired

      c. Fox

  B. Tracking

    1. Hounds

      a. Bloodhounds

      b. Basset Hounds

    2. Doberman Pinschers

    3. Saint Bernards

  C. Herding

    1. Collie

    2. Bearded Collie

    3. Sheepdog

  D. Guarding

    1. Rottweilers

    2. German Shepherds

    3. Doberman Pinschers

II. House Pets

  A. Small Breeds

    1. Shih Tzus

    2. Lhasa apsos

    3. Toy poodles

  B. Medium Breeds

    1. Cocker spaniels

    2. Scotch terriers

  C. Large Breeds

    1. Airedales

    2. Alaskan malamutes

    3. Siberian Huskies

(Continue in this manner until you have outlined all the categories you have chosen.)

Outlining Practice

Outline practice is fun, and it could turn you into an outlining expert. For this outline you won't even need to look in any books to find the information. You already have it in your head. You are going to write an outline about yourself. Here is an example just to give you an idea, but you can use any topics and subtopics you want. Just be sure to include at least five topics in your outline.

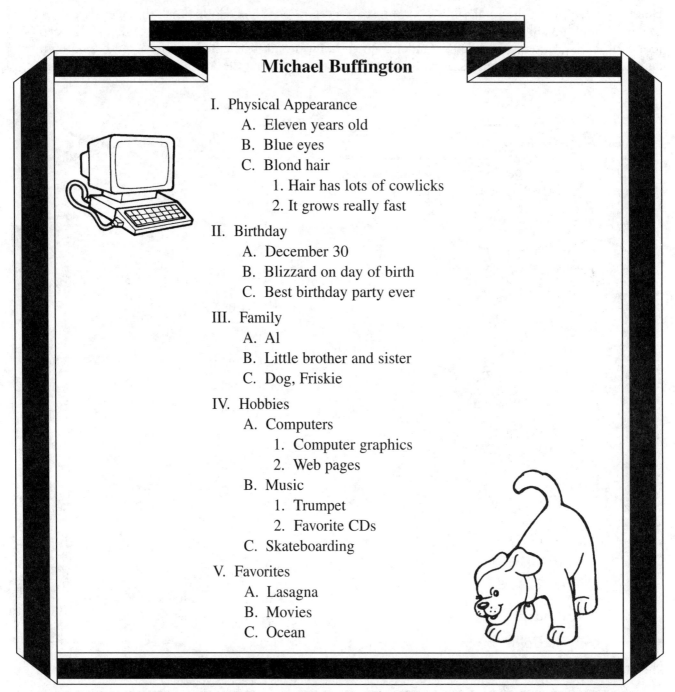

Michael Buffington

I. Physical Appearance
    A. Eleven years old
    B. Blue eyes
    C. Blond hair
       1. Hair has lots of cowlicks
       2. It grows really fast

II. Birthday
    A. December 30
    B. Blizzard on day of birth
    C. Best birthday party ever

III. Family
    A. Al
    B. Little brother and sister
    C. Dog, Friskie

IV. Hobbies
    A. Computers
       1. Computer graphics
       2. Web pages
    B. Music
       1. Trumpet
       2. Favorite CDs
    C. Skateboarding

V. Favorites
    A. Lasagna
    B. Movies
    C. Ocean

Now, take out a piece of paper and write your own outline all about you! Add pictures of you doing some of the activities in the outline.

Facts and Opinions

When you write a research paper, you must be very careful to stick to the facts. A research paper is written to give people information that is true or that can be proven true.

Is this a fact?

"France is the best place in the world to live."

Whether you agree or not, it is just someone's opinion. It is not a fact.

In the blanks before each sentence below, write F for fact or O for opinion.

_____ 1. The moon orbits the earth.

_____ 2. The moon is inspirational to all who see it.

_____ 3. A banana tastes disgusting.

_____ 4. A banana is a fruit.

_____ 5. Abraham Lincoln was killed.

_____ 6. Abraham Lincoln was the best president.

_____ 7. Canada has the most beautiful lakes in the world.

_____ 8. Canada has many lakes.

_____ 9. Red and yellow mixed together make orange.

_____ 10. Orange is the prettiest color.

Many plants have thorns. (fact)

Thorny plants are not good in gardens. (opinion)

Now write one fact and one opinion about your school.

1. Fact: _____

2. Opinion: _____

Charts and Diagrams

Adding a few charts or diagrams will make your report more interesting. To begin, brainstorm for ideas. For example, if you are writing a report on ice cream, here are a few ideas for some charts and diagrams:

Brainstorm in the space below by listing additional ideas for charts and diagrams about ice cream (or the topic about which you are writing).

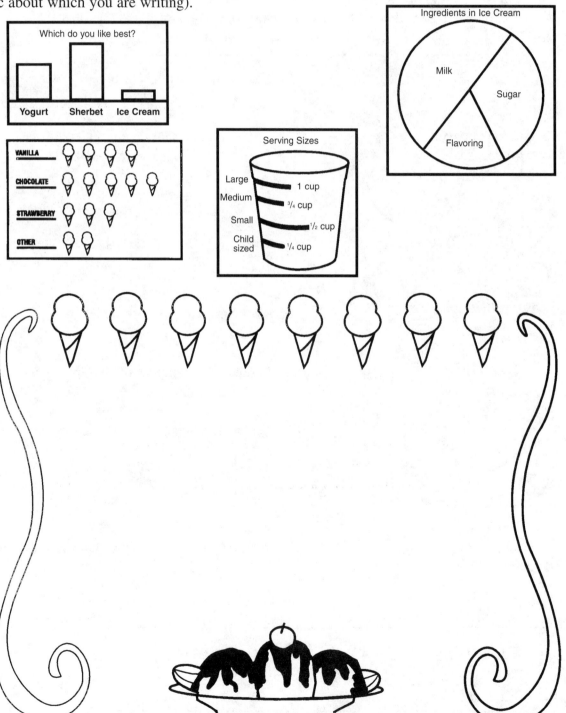

The Picture Report

It is said that a picture is worth a thousand words. Whether that is a fact or an opinion, it is true that a picture can say a lot. This is your opportunity to share all you have learned about your topic with pictures and words.

Materials

- a collection of nonfiction library picture books
- index cards, any size
- 8½" x 11" (22 cm x 25 cm) scratch paper
- unlined, and lined 8½" x 11" (22 cm x 28 cm) notebook paper
- pens, pencils, markers, crayons, etc.
- report folder

Directions

1. To begin, look at as many nonfiction picture books as you can. Notice how the nonfiction picture books are full of information about a topic. For example, you might find a nonfiction picture book about puppies. You will see that each page has a large illustration that shows what the words describe.

2. Use index cards to take notes just as you would for a regular research report. When you have enough notes, it's time to plan your picture report.

3. Plan how many pages you will create. Your teacher will give you guidelines about the length of your picture report and how to write a table of contents and a bibliography.

When puppies are born, their eyes are closed. They won't be opening them for a week or two. They use their sense of smell to find their mother.

4. Take the information you wish to use, put it in logical order, and decide which pages will contain what information. (You will probably want one brief paragraph per page, but keep your illustrations in mind as you plan; you won't want two illustrations in a row that are the same or nearly the same.)

5. Using scratch paper, divide each page into four boxes. Number each box to match the pages of your picture report. In each box, include a quick sketch of the illustration and the information that will go on each page. Make changes until you have it the way you want it. Then draw each illustration as planned on notebook paper. Be sure to fill up the page with your art, leaving only enough room for the words. With ink, add the words to each page.

6. When your pages are completed, put them in order in a report folder.

7. Don't forget to give it a title page, put art on the cover, and remember "Written and Illustrated by _____."

The Writing Process

When we write a research report, there are steps we take to get from the idea to the finished product. Sometimes we take a step more than once, sometimes we go back or forward in a slightly different order, but the basic steps are as follows. As you work through these steps in writing your report, refer to this list often.

Prewriting

Thinking, reading, researching, note-taking, listing, brainstorming, outlining, clustering, and anything else that will help you to think about and plan what you will be writing.

First Draft Writing

Write a "sloppy copy." Take all your ideas and plans and just write, letting your ideas and words flow onto the paper. Don't worry too much about spelling or grammar when you write a first draft; instead, concentrate on what you want to say and the order in which you want to say it.

Response

This is the stage when you have others read or hear what you've written, and you get a response from them. Do they understand what you are saying? Are you being clear and interesting? Listen carefully to find out what you are doing well and what needs more work.

Revision

This is the time to look more carefully at what you have written and make changes. You might change some words, rearrange some sentences, move some paragraphs around, add some details or important information you might have left out.

Editing and Rewriting

Before this stage, you may have had the opportunity to ask others to check your work for spelling and grammar errors. If not, be sure to check carefully. Writers often miss these kinds of mistakes. Check spelling with a dictionary. Read your report aloud; you'll find more mistakes that way. Have a parent look at your report, too. Make all the changes needed.

Evaluation

In this stage, your teacher and/or your classmates will let you know what they think of your report. Your teacher will evaluate your report to make sure you completed it according to the directions given to you.

Publishing

Once your report is presented to others, it is considered to be published (so pat yourself on the back). In addition, it may be published by appearing on a bulletin board or in a class book or newsletter.

Research Report Format

____ Typing, Printing, or Handwriting Your Report:

Start with a fresh typewriter ribbon or computer printer cartridge so the type will be dark and easy to read. Use black ink on 8½" x 11" (22 cm x 28 cm) unlined white paper. (Thin, erasable paper smears). Set for double space to leave a space between each line. Write on only one side of the paper; do not draw or glue anything on the back of any page. Pictures, charts, or diagrams go on a separate page. With your teacher's permission to handwrite your report, write carefully and neatly. Use white correction fluid sparingly. If there are many mistakes, write the page over.

____ Margins:

Leave one-inch (2.5 cm) margins around the top, bottom, and sides of each page, even where there is no writing. Indent five spaces at the beginning of each paragraph. For quotations of three or more lines, indent ten spaces on each side and omit the quotation marks. For example:

> *The park ranger at Sequoia National Park reported that there are more bears in the park this year due to extra heavy rains. With the rivers and streams flooded, the bears come to the lower elevations to look for food.*

____ Title:

Your teacher will tell you if you need a title page. If so, only the title is written in capital letters. Then, on separate lines write your name, the name of the class or subject, your teacher's name, and the date (see page 34). If a title page is not required, the title goes at the top of the first page of your report.

____ Page Numbers:

Beginning with the second page, write the page number in the upper right-hand corner of each page.

____ Art, Charts, Pictures, etc.:

For some charts or tables, you may wish to leave space on the page to draw or glue a chart that goes with the text. Or you can write in your report, "see chart number 3," and include all your charts, tables, photos, and art at the end of your report.

____ Folders and Covers:

Bind your report in a paper or a lightweight plastic report cover. Punch holes in the left side of the pages. Be sure your report can be read after you assemble it. Avoid plastic sleeves for written pages. Art, pictures, charts, etc., can be placed inside three-hole sheet protectors and then into the report binder.

The Title Page

If your teacher tells you to include a title page with your report, here is how it's done. Look at the examples below. Follow your teacher's directions. Ask before you add artwork to your title page.

THE HISTORY OF
SPACE EXPLORATION

by Javier Monteros

Social Studies, Period 3

Mrs. Harrington

March 22, 1999

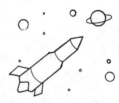

SHORE BIRDS

by Kesha Clarke

Science, Period 2

Mr. Benincosa

February 7, 1998

CHILDREN OF THE
UNDERGROUND RAILROAD

by Meagan Hansen

Social Studies, Period 5

Mrs. Harvey

May 3, 2000

Writing the Introduction

A good introduction grabs the reader's attention, introduces the topic (your main idea statement) and follows briefly with the subtopics to be presented in the report. For a short, five- to eight-paragraph report, a one-paragraph introduction will do. For a report of four or more pages, your introduction may be a page or more long. Notice how this is done in the following example:

> *The Anasazi, known as "The Ancient Ones," were a highly developed and prosperous group of Native Americans who lived a long time ago. They built spectacular two- and three-story homes and round towers in the sides of cliffs. They practiced farming and made beautiful pottery and bows and arrows. There were thousands of Anasazi who were also skilled at other crafts, including blanket, making stonework, basket weaving, and jewelry and tool making. Tourists looking at their handiwork today realize that the Anasazi were both artistic and practical.*

From this introduction, a list of subtopics to be presented in the report can easily be made:

- meaning of *"The Ancient Ones"*
- Anasazi *homes and architecture*
- Anasazi *farming and food*
- Anasazi *crafts*
- *archaeologists' ideas* about the Anasazi

Introduction Work Sheet

My main idea statement is _____

The subtopics I will write about in my report are these:

1. _____

2. _____

3. _____

4. _____

5. _____

On another paper, write your introduction. Start with your main idea statement and then briefly introduce the subtopics you listed above. It's okay to look at your outline, cluster, note cards, and the example above. Don't go into detail yet; just be sure to mention each subtopic. Check to see if your introduction flows well from one idea to the next. When your rough draft introduction says what you want it to say, ask a classmate for a response before you turn it in to your teacher.

Topic Sentences

Your report needs to have a "body." The body of the report is all the subtopic paragraphs that come after your introduction and before your conclusion. Each of these paragraphs needs to start with its own topic sentence to tell the reader what that paragraph will be about. In a report on the Anasazi, some of the main paragraph topic sentences would be as follows:

- The Anasazi built spectacular two- and three-story dwellings in the sides of the cliffs.

- In addition to hunting, the Anasazi developed advanced forms of farming.

- The Anasazi made beautiful pottery and other practical, artistic handicrafts.

Write a topic sentence for each of the following paragraphs:

1. Pasta is quick and easy to cook. All that is needed is a big pot, water, and heat. It is full of carbohydrates and low in fat. People could eat pasta almost everyday. Because there are so many different kinds of pasta and sauces, it would never get boring.

2. A person has to be in good shape to swim in the ocean. The currents and waves are always changing, so a swimmer has to be prepared. Swimming in a current takes more muscle power than swimming in a pool where the water is not in constant motion. The changing waves and sea life make the ocean a more interesting place to swim.

3. Guinea pigs are easy to take care of. All they need is a cage, a wheel, some sawdust, food, and water. They're soft and cuddly. They don't take up much space. They don't bark or make any loud noises. You can carry them anywhere. They are funny to watch. They'll stuff their cheeks full of grapes, wash themselves, and run around and around on their wheels.

Write in the subject for each topic sentence below. Then on another paper, write a four- to six-sentence paragraph for each of these topic sentences, filling in your own details.

1. _____ make great pets.

2. _____ is a good thing to do in the summer.

3. _____ is a difficult job.

Body Paragraphs

The "body" of your report is the largest and most important part. This is where you will put most of the information you've worked so long and hard to research. Use your outline or cluster to decide how many body paragraphs you will need. Move your note card piles around as you try to arrange them in some logical subtopic order. Remember, you will need to write a topic sentence to begin each paragraph in the body of your report. For example, for a report on "The Sandwich," the student wrote the following topic sentences to begin each of his body paragraphs:

> The first sandwich was invented by a man in a hurry by the name of The Earl of Sandwich.
>
> After the Earl's idea caught on, people began to develop their own versions of the sandwich.
>
> Foreign influence on the sandwich can be seen in the taco, the burrito, the egg roll, the falafel pita, the calzone, and even the pizza.
>
> The hamburger became the king of sandwiches in the 50s.
>
> The East Coast influenced sandwich making with the hoagie, the submarine, and the corned beef on rye.
>
> The hot dog represents a mixture of cultures.

Now get out your stacks of note cards and your outline or cluster. In the space below, write each of your body paragraphs' topic sentences in the order you plan to use them.

Topic sentence #1: _____

_____

Topic sentence #2: _____

_____

Topic sentence #3: _____

_____

Topic sentence #4: _____

_____

Topic sentence #5: _____

_____

Topic sentence #6: _____

_____

Giving Credit Where Credit Is Due

It is okay to use another person's ideas, phrases, or words in your report, but when you do, you need to give credit to that person. You don't need to give credit for everything you write in your report. For information that is common knowledge, such as "Mt. Everest is the tallest mountain in the world. It is 29,028 feet (8,848 meters) tall," you don't need to give credit since this is information that can be found pretty much anywhere. But if you write, "Maybe all the dinosaurs went to another planet; maybe they went to Jupiter or Mars" because you read a book where the author, being imaginative, was wondering if the dinosaurs went to these planets, you should give credit to the author of these ideas. Here is how it would look in your report:

> "Many people speculate about what happened to the dinosaurs. Some
> say a giant meteor collided with the earth and changed the environment.
> One children's book author playfully asks if they went to " . . . another
> planet? Maybe they're on Jupiter or Mars" (Most, 3).

The author of the book *Whatever Happened to the Dinosaurs*? is Bernard Most, so after the part that is quoted from the book, you put the author's last name and the page number you used. Then, at the end of your report, you will include the author and his book in the bibliography. Notice that the punctuation for your sentence comes after the parentheses. You should give credit even when you don't quote the author directly, such as follows:

> When a starfish is young, it has a tail and floats in the ocean. When it is
> grown, it loses its tail and lives on the bottom of the ocean (Straker, 11).

The author above was not quoted directly, but so many of her words were used that credit needs to be given. And, of course, you should always give credit when you quote directly:

> "Uncle Henry never laughed. He worked hard from morning till night
> and did not know what joy was. He was gray also, from his long beard
> to his rough boots, and he looked stern and solemn, and rarely spoke"
> (Baum, 12).

Any questions?

What if the book I'm using doesn't have an author?

In that case, use the title instead of the author's last name. If the title is long, you can shorten it. The important thing is for readers to be able to find it in your bibliography.

The article I am using has no page numbers; it's just one page. What should I do?

You don't need to put a page number if you use a one-page article or articles from encyclopedias.

That's all there is to it. The author's last name, or the title of the article or book if there is no author, and the page number, or no page number if it is just one page or from an encyclopedia.

Writing the Conclusion

"And in conclusion . . . ."

Have you ever heard a speaker say those words and then continue on and on? Maybe some people just don't know how to come to a conclusion but you will know how! The conclusion means THIS IS THE END! It is the final paragraph of your report.

Your conclusion needs to give a brief summary of what you covered (your main points) in your report. Here are the things that you should include in your conclusion. You don't always need to include all of them, but include as many as you possibly can. Those items which you should always include in a conclusion have an asterisk (*) listed after them.

---

1. A summary of your main points *

2. Your opinion about your research

3. What you learned from writing the report

4. Why the subject is important to you

5. Where the reader can find more information

6. A strong ending sentence that will make a lasting impression *

Here are several short concluding paragraphs (yours may be longer, depending on the length of your report). After you read each sample, give it a grade—pass or fail. Give it a *pass* if you think it meets the requirements of a concluding paragraph. Give it a *fail* if you think it is not quite good enough. Give it a *pass+* if you think it is especially good.

_____ 1. You know what I think now if you've read my report, and so now I will simply say, "The End."

_____ 2. And so, it is clear that space exploration must go on because it can benefit all through the discoveries made, the research it provides, and the sense of togetherness it gives to the people of the earth. Someday I hope to be an astronaut, and one day you just might visit your grandchildren on another planet!

_____ 3. In this research report I have written about dogs and all the things that they do as workers and pets. I have also researched cats and other pets; it was really interesting but I didn't put those things in my report, as you can see. The reason that dogs are important to me is because I really like them. I hope you enjoyed reading my report!

_____ 4. I am now finished writing about some old movies that are really interesting. I hope you liked this too. I think the old movies are much better than the new ones.

The Bibliography

The bibliography is the last page of your report! It will be easy if you wrote the sources you used on your source note cards. Simply make a list of your sources in alphabetical order by the author's last name. If no author is given, alphabetize by the title (skipping *a*, *an* and *the*).

Below is an example of a bibliography in alphabetical order. On the blank, write whether each is a **book**, **software**, **magazine**, **encyclopedia**, **video** or **Internet**. Then discuss your answers with the class. Keep this page to look at when you write your own bibliography.

Bibliography

1. _____ *Anasazi, The Ancient Ones.* A National Park film, Cortez, CO 81321.

2. _____ Baum, L. Frank. *The Wizard of Oz.* Rand McNally & Co., 1956.

3. _____ *Boy Scouts of America.* Indian Lore. 1992.

4. _____ Hixson, Susan. *Internet in the Classroom* [Online].
   http://www.indirect.com/www/dhixson/class.html.

5. _____ Julian, Judith L, *Plot Lions*. Vers. 1.3. Writing Software, Inc., 1990. PC-DOS 2.0, 256 KB, disk.

6. _____ *Mapquest.* http://www.mapquest.com.

7. _____ Most, Bernard. *Whatever Happened to the Dinosaurs?* Harcourt Brace Jovanovich, 1984.

8. _____ Pettingill, Olin Sewall, Jr. "Falcon and Falconry." *World Book Encyclopedia*. 1980.

9. _____ Straker, Joan Ann. *Animals That Live in the Sea*. National Geographic Society, 1978.

10. _____ Sunset Books and Sunset Magazine. *New Western Garden Book*. Lane Publishing Co., 1979.

Bibliographies are single spaced, with a space between entries. The first line of each entry begins at the left margin, but the second line is indented five spaces. This is called a "hanging indent" on the computer. On handwritten reports, titles need to be underlined in place of italics. Refer to the above examples, if needed, especially for correct order and punctuation. Put a period after the author, the title, and the publishing date.

Multimedia Reports

If you have done research on the Internet or a CD-ROM encyclopedia, you are already familiar with multimedia. When you are clicking the various icons and buttons on the computer screen, having articles open up, or seeing videos or hearing sound, you are "reading" a multimedia report. You can create one, too! Just follow these suggestions:

- Use a multimedia software program such as *HyperStudio* or any similar school program.

- Use the tutorial and the manual to become familiar with the program. Try creating a few hyperstacks (organized information). It's quite easy.

- Take a look at your notes, outlines, and clusters. Decide what information you would like to include in a multimedia research report.

- Select five important subtopics and five bits of interesting information for each.

- Using large note cards, plan your *hyperstack* beginning with your home page. (It is also the title page). Include the title of your report, your name, the subject, class, and your teacher's name on this card. Add graphics to make the page interesting.

- Add five buttons to direct readers to the other cards in your stack. If you researched "frontier pioneers," you might have a button that leads to a "history" card: why they went west, where they went, events. You could have a button that leads to "pioneer food" and tell what was hunted, harvested, and cooked along the trail, and what they did when they ran out of food. "Pioneer amusements" could describe what they did for recreation: dancing, music, games, toys, etc. All of your main headings would be represented.

- Once you have your cards organized, you can get really creative. Design the buttons any way you want: scroll for more information; add pictures, photographs, even video from an encyclopedia program or other source; add pioneer music or a personal interview to add sound to your report.

Anyone looking at your report should be able to click on any button to go to any page and return to revisit any page. On another paper, write some interesting things we might see, read, and experience in your multimedia report for each of these topics:

Pioneers of the Western Frontier

1. Why They Went West
2. Dangers and Defenses
3. Pioneer Food
4. Pioneer Clothing
5. Pioneer Innovations That Opened Up the West

6. Games and Toys
7. Dance and Music
8. Storytelling

The Research Poster

A research poster is like a one-page report! But what a one-page research report it is! First of all, it is a large piece of paper. In fact, it is a poster full of information! It will have one dramatically large, simply drawn illustration as its most important feature. You will need to research to complete it.

Materials

- a large poster board
- markers, pencils, paints, glue, etc.
- resources (encyclopedias, reference books)
- index cards

Directions

1. You will need to take notes so you will have plenty of facts on your topic. If your topic is the human body, for example, take notes on the names of the organs, muscles, bones, etc. If your topic is a country, province, or state, you will want to pay close attention to features like lakes, mountains, etc.

2. Decide what you will put on your poster. If it will be the shape of a human or the outline of a country, sketch it first on a large sheet of paper and see how it will fit on your poster. If your topic is volcanoes, you may want to draw the outline of a large volcano so that you can show what it is like on the inside.

3. Draw your poster illustration. Only do the outline at first to be sure there is plenty of room for your facts.

4. Add your facts with lines pointing to what the facts are naming. Once you have all your facts on the poster, you can add more detail and color to the illustration.

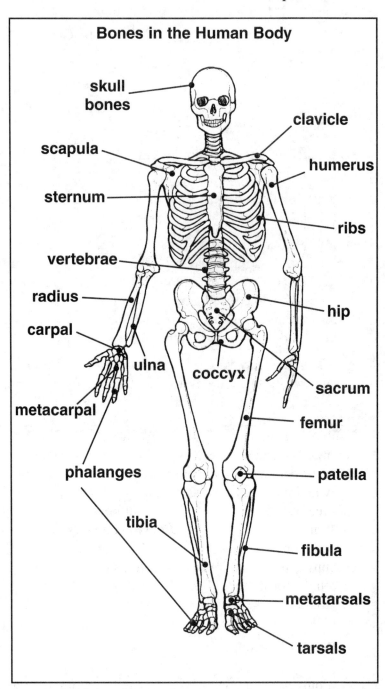

Extension: Create a 3-D relief map of a country, state, or province by putting salt and flour dough or purchased clay onto tagboard or Masonite. Shape and label the mountains, valleys, and bodies of water.

Add Zip to Your Report!

You have worked hard. You have read many books, taken many notes, written many pages, and learned many new things. Your report is full of interesting facts. Many of your classmates will learn new things because of your hard work. Here are some ways to share even more of what you have learned and to make your research report even more successful.

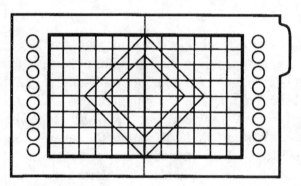

Games

Create a game based upon the topic of your research report. The simplest way to do this would be to draw a board game on the inside of a file folder. If you wrote a report about whales, for example, you could create a board game in which the players (different species of whales) are trying to be the first to migrate to their summer home. When players land on a space, they could do what it says on that space: move ahead or back, answer a question about whales (you can create a stack of whale trivia questions to be answered), go back to assist another whale, get beached, etc. Make your game colorful, create markers (try clay or salt and flour dough), add a die or make one, and ask your teacher to help you laminate the board for your game. When you are not playing it, you can fold it and attach a zip-close bag to hold the cards and pieces.

Activities and Demonstrations

Lead your classmates in an activity to help them learn about your subject. If you wrote about volcanoes, you could teach them how to create their own volcanoes. Ask your teacher or librarian for help in finding the directions. Go over them carefully and practice at home with a parent to help. When you are ready, talk to your teacher about how you will demonstrate in class and when. Should you simply demonstrate one volcanic eruption? Can you divide the class into groups and have each group create its own volcano while you demonstrate? With any activity or demonstration, be sure to discuss it completely with your teacher, and he or she can help you prepare the materials and set a time.

Quizzes

Create a quiz for your classmates. It can be an oral quiz or a written one. Whatever kind it is, be sure to make it interesting and fun. You can even add some funny questions to make it interesting. On a written quiz, add some drawings. For an oral quiz, use some visual aids. Be sure to share the information with your classmates before the quiz.

Add Zip to Your Report! *(cont.)*

Word Search

Using the most important words from your topic, create a word search puzzle for your classmates. If you need help, ask your teacher for a sample of a word search puzzle. Use graph paper to help keep your lines straight and write your words up, down, sideways, and backwards. Fill in the spaces with letters that don't spell anything at all. Your teacher can help you make copies to give to your classmates.

Crossword Puzzles

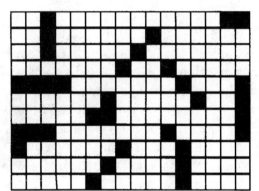

First, make a list of words from your report that you would like to use. Using graph paper, cut out letters, or use letter tiles from a word board game. Arrange the words until you can find ways for them to intersect at common letters. When you have an arrangement with five to ten words, write it down so you don't lose it. With graph paper, outline the squares you will be using. Place a number in the beginning letter square of each word. Leave the squares blank. Now write a question, hint, riddle, or clue for each word. Write these at the bottom of your graph paper. Make sure they are numbered to match the spaces on the puzzle. Double check to make sure you have spelled correctly, that you have the right number of squares for each word, and that each clue's number correctly matches the number on the puzzle. Make copies to share with your classmates.

Oral Presentations

You can present the information in your report by simply summarizing it to your classmates and sharing the illustrations, charts, diagrams, maps, etc. You can bring in food or give a cooking demonstration if your report is about a culture or country.

If your report is about flight, you can give a presentation in paper airplane folding and talk about aerodynamics.

If you write your report with a team or partner, you can give a panel discussion where each of you is prepared to share certain areas of the report. You each become experts and answer classmates' questions.

If a classmate wrote a report about a similar topic, you can prepare a debate for the class. If you write a report on football, for example, and a classmate writes a report on soccer, you can debate about which sport is better.

Helpful Tips

1. Think about who you are writing for.

    • What do they want or need to know?

    • What will be interesting to them?

    • What will they want to learn?

    • How can I help them learn about my subject in an interesting way?

2. Think about what information would make your report more understandable and what information could be left out.

3. Give yourself lots of time to work on each part of your report. This will reduce the stress and make it a more enjoyable experience.

4. If your report seems too long, with too many subtopics, narrow your subject down more. What seems less important and might be taken out?

5. Avoid using "I" or "you" or "we" when you write a research report. Write in third person (he, she, it, they, etc.) Write like a newspaper reporter. If you need help with this, try reading some front-page news writing.

6. In some kinds of reports, you can give an opinion; in some you should not. If you can give an opinion, it belongs in your conclusion, not in the body of your report. Check with your teacher.

7. If you are doing your report on the computer, where can you add visual effects (bullets, borders, boldface, font changes, graphics, pictures, charts, etc.)?

8. Make your final draft and your finishing touches as polished as you can. This is the end product of all of your efforts for many weeks. Be sure it shows how hard you have worked!

Final Checklist

Before you turn in your report, write "yes" or "no" before each of the following questions. These are many of the things your teacher will be looking for in a good report. This is your last chance to make it your best effort.

_____ Does it have a good introduction? Does it get the reader's attention and introduce your topics?

_____ Does it have enough information and interesting details in the body?

_____ Does it have a good conclusion? Does it summarize your important points and leave the reader with a lasting impression?

_____ Check the paragraphs. Do they each begin with the topic sentence? Are they arranged in order?

_____ Check the wording. Have you used your own words and given credit when you've used someone else's?

_____ Is it interesting? Have you used precise words, strong verbs, good descriptions? Have you added illustrations, charts, graphs, and maps?

_____ Is it accurate? Check your facts for missing information. Check your spelling and grammar.

_____ Does it have a title page? Does the title page meet the requirements your teacher gave you?

_____ Does it have a bibliography? Be sure the bibliography is complete and in the correct form.

_____ Is it neat and easy to read? Is it typed in dark ink and double spaced? Or is it hand-written in black or blue ink and legible? Do any pages need to be rewritten for neatness? Are the pages numbered? Are there margins of one inch all around?

_____ Have you patted yourself on the back for your extraordinary effort and successful accomplishment of your first research report project?

Resources

Ackermann, Ernest. *Learning to Use the Internet—An Introduction with Examples and Exercises*. Franklin, Beedle & Associates, 1995.

Butler, Mark. *How to Use the Internet*. Ziff-Davis Press, 1994.

Fowler, Allan. *The Library of Congress*. Children's Press, 1996.

Gardner, Paul. *Internet for Teachers and Parents*. Teacher Created Resources, 1996.

Giagnocavo, Gregory, Tim McLain, and Vince DiStefano. *Educator's Internet Companion*. Wentworth Worldwide Media, Inc., 1995.

Haag, Tim. *Internet for Kids*. Teacher Created Resources, 1996.

Hardendorff, Jeanne B. *Libraries and How to Use Them.* Franklin Watts, 1979.

McLain, Tim and Vince DiStefano. *Educator's Worldwide Web Tour Guide*. Wentworth Worldwide Media, Inc., 1995.

Null, Kathleen Christopher. *How to Give a Presentation*. Teacher Created Resources, 1998.

Pederson, Ted & Francis Moss. *Internet for Kids! A Beginner's Guide to Surfing the Net*. Price Stern Sloan, Inc., 1995.

Periera, Linda. *Computers Don't Byte*. Teacher Created Resources, 1996.

Salzman, Marian & Robert Pondiscio. *Kids On-Line*. Avon Books, 1995.

Salzman, Marian & Robert Pondiscio. *The Ultimate On-Line Homework Helper*. Avon Books, 1996.

Web Sites

American Memory. http://rs6.loc.gov/amhome.html

The Children's Literature Home Page. http://www.ucalgary.ca/~dkbrown/index.html

Children's Online Literature Gopher. gopher://lib.nmsu.edu/11/.subjects/education/.childlit

Classroom Connect. http://www.classroom.net/

Cool School Tools. http://www.bham.lib.al.us/cooltools/

The Electronic Zoo. http://netvet.wustl.edu/history.htm

Encyclopedia Britannica Online. http://www.eb.com

Exploratorium. http://www.exploratorium.edu

The Internet Public Library. http://ipl.sils.umich.edu

Kids on the Web. http://www.zen.org:80/brendan/kids.html

Le Louvre. http://mistral.enst.fr/~pioch/louvre/

Mapquest. http://www.mapquest.com/

Museum of Paleontology. http://ucmp1.berkeley.edu/ehibittext/entrance.html

NASA/JPL Imaging Radar Home Page. http://southport.jpl.nasa.gov

National Geographic Online. http://www.nationalgeographic.com

Online Educational Resources. http://quest.arc.nasa.gov/oer/

Spacelink. spacelink.msfc.nasa.gov

Virtual Museums. http://www.icom.org/vlmp/

Virtual Tourist. http://wings.buffalo.edu/world/vt2/

The White House. http://www.whitehouse.gov

Search Engines

(Note: Become familiar with search engines before attempting to teach your students. Be sure the computers you are using have blocking software such as *NetNanny* or *Cyber Patrol*. Carefully monitor students. Keywords may have inappropriate meanings. Search engines will list all sites for that keyword, whatever its intended meaning.)

Alta Vista	*Infoseek*	*Magellan*
http://altavista.digital.com	http://guide.infoseek.com	http://www.mckinley.com
Excite	*Lycos*	*Yahoo*
http://www.excite.com	http://www.lycos.com	http://www.yahoo.com

Note: Web site addresses were accurate at the time of this printing.

Answer Key

Page 4—What Is a Research Report?
Accept any beginning attempts to narrow a subject. This is a first-step exercise; more narrowing will occur with Choosing a Subject, page 5)

Page 5—Choosing a Subject
Accept any reasonable narrowing of subjects, e.g.:
1. trains, airlines, ferry boats
2. ants, bees, butterflies
3. specific holiday from Kwanzaa to Veteran's Day, cultural or foreign holidays
4. A specific plant or function of plants
5. The origins of the national park system, a specific park.

Page 6—Writing Prompts
Accept appropriate responses that are creative, use the 5 W's and 1 H, and use the senses.

Page 12—Finding Books on Library Shelves
1. Fine Arts, sports, 700–799, 2nd
2. Literature, poetry, 800–899, 1st
3. General Works, atlas, 000–099, 6th
4. Fine Arts, music, 700–799 2nd
5. Pure Sciences, math, 500–599, 3rd
6. History, biography, 900–999, 1st
7. Language, dictionary, 400–499, 4th
8. Social Science, government 300–399, 4th
9. Applied Science, cooking, 600–699, 3rd
10. Religion, mythology, 200–299, 5th

*Note: Most topics can also be found on the sixth floor.

Page 13—Finding Books on Library Shelves (*cont.*)
1. 501
   K
2. 530
   B
3. 530
   T
4. 546
   I
5. 579
   P
6. 581
   C

7. 592
   N

Page 17—Using Encyclopedia Volumes
photography, Mo–Qu
dinosaurs, Cu–Ex
Hawaii, Gy–Ju
chocolate, Aa–Cu
rattlesnakes, Qu–Ty
lightning, Ju–Mo
wildflowers, We–Z
computers, Aa–Cu
Beatles, The, Aa–Cu
volcanoes, Ty–We
space shuttle, Qu–Ty
gorillas, Ex-Gy

Page 19—Card and Computer Catalogs
The Napping House (title)
oceans (subject)
skiing (subject)
Mark Twain (author)
The Black Stallion (title)
India (subject)
The Bridge to Terabithia (title)
computers (subject)
Theodore Taylor (author)
Island of the Blue Dolphins (title)

Page 22—The Main Idea Statement
Accept appropriate subject narrowing such as
Basketball—the history of basketball, women in . . .
Space—the space shuttle, Exploration of Mars, the *Mir*
Computers—history, in the classroom, at home
Horses—Working horses, show horses, early horses
Ice Cream—worldwide, history of, how it's made
Check students' main idea statements before they go any further.

Page 28—Outlining Practice
Check to be sure that students have outlined at least five topics on the subject of themselves.

Page 29—Facts and Opinions
1. Fact
2. Opinion
3. Opinion
4. Fact
5. Fact
6. Opinion
7. Opinion

8. Fact
9. Fact
10. Opinion
Accept appropriate facts and opinions about the school.

Page 36—Topic Sentences
Write the topic sentences: Accept any appropriate responses similar to
1. Pasta is a quick, economical, healthy, and interesting food.
2. It's better to swim in the ocean than in a pool.
3. Guinea pigs make great pets.

Write a subject; write a paragraph: Accept any reasonable responses that are complete paragraphs supporting their topic sentences.

Page 39—Writing the Conclusion
1. Fail—lacks a summary, a concluding sentence, ending fizzles, etc.
2. Pass+ —best but not perfect. How could it be made better?
3. Fail—vague, rambling
4. Fail—not enough information

Page 40—The Bibliography
1. video
2. book
3. book
4. Internet
5. software
6. Internet
7. book
8. encyclopedia
9. book
10. book

Page 41—Multimedia Reports
Accept any reasonable responses.